MY REFLECTIONS ON LIFE,
A BOOK OF POETRY AND THOUGHTS

A LEAF FELL UPON MY HEART

SCOTT REALL

© 2024 by Restore Small Groups

Cover image by John McCann on Unsplash

Cover and interior design by Linda Bourdeaux/thedesigndesk.com

Interior photos by Unsplash—Sixteen Miles Out (pg iv), Hannah Tims (pg 3), Nathan Dumlao (pg 4), S Tsuchiya (pg 7), Cody Black (pg 8), Mathilde Langevin (Page 11), Andrew Ling (pg 15), Anthony Cantin (pg 16), Danielle Dolson (pg 19), Casey Horner (pg 23), Logan Weaver (pg 25), Jennifer Burk Age 26), Erik Witsoe (pg 29), Benjamin Voros (pg 30), John Towner (pg 33), Leonid (pg 34), Mira Ohoro (pg 37), Aaron Burden (pg 38)

All rights reserved. No portion of this book may be reproduced, stored in a retrieval system, or transmitted in any form or by any means—electronic, mechanical, photocopy, recording, scanning, or any other—except for brief quotations in critical reviews or articles, without the prior written permission of the publisher.

To find a Restore Small Group near you, please visit the following website: restoresmallgroups.org.

If you would like to invite Scott to speak to your church, community organization, or event, please visit restoresmallgroups.org

If you would like to donate to Restore Small Groups to help support the life-changing work of this ministry, please visit restoresmallgroups.org.

ISBN: 979-8-9889747-9-6

This is dedicated to all the friends, staff, volunteers and donors of Restore who have made this life-changing ministry possible to impact the world with hope and healing of Christ. There have been special people that God has put in my path to inspire me to write these poems and books—to all of you, I say Thank You.

A THOUGHT OF YOU

The sounds of a new day
Sing in the voices
Of the morning birds
My awareness of time and place
Slowly awakens from my sleep
And a thought of you dances
Through my mind
A dream or reality blends
Into one
And a warm memory unfolds
Inside my soul
With a thought of you.

TO LOVE THE LONGING

I am aware of this longing in my heart
It remains like a damp mist
Of a hopeless dream
That awaits my days
I seek and chase the fleeting light
But it fades from my sight
Before it can be birthed
And arise
To become
To love the longing
The reprisal of my heart.

TO BE ME

Often in my days
I wander
Through thoughts and memories
And fading dreams
I struggle with being me
To know this heart of tender space
To feel alone
So different
So strange
Does anyone know
Does anyone care
How hard it can be
To be me?

SUNSET

The day gently closes its door
The last beams of sunlight
Slip across my floor
A soft color that blends
Beneath the frames of the day
The day passes into the shade
A sweet sad sigh
My heart's last reply
And I say
Goodbye.

TO BE

What is this that I see
This vision
To be
The touch of a dream
Awakens in me
Longing to become
Longing to be free
Let it go
Let it all go
To Be!

I AM WITH YOU

A memory has come from your smile
and the sound of your voice.
I recall them now as one heart... one soul.
And I see you... I feel you...
I am with you.

HOPE MAY
KEEP A MAN
ALIVE WITHIN
TIME...
BUT LOVE
MAKES A MAN
FEEL ALIVE
WITHIN TIME.

REBIRTH

To this morning light
I awake
To the sounds of a new day
Singing a song to life
It has come
Bringing my Rebirth
A new Hope has been born
My soul leaps to see
The possible in me
To be...

DO YOU SEE

There is a heart

That has courageously appeared

Upon your porch

It trembles with anticipation

For you to greet

Do you see its scars

From its past searches

For the longings of loves refrain

Will you know the heights

It has climbed to brave again

To hope again

Do you see

There is a heart

That has courageously appeared

Upon your porch

Do you see?

YOU APPEARED

The morning sun glanced over the horizon
I looked beyond the lines of daylight
that were just being born
And there you appeared
Born of my hopes and prayers
The hearts dream
To believe to see
The moment you first appeared

BEYOND

Beyond all that I can touch
Beyond all that I can see
Beyond the horizon of all that I can hope
A dream will come to appear
And so will end
All of my fears.

MY MORNING WINDOW

I gaze through my morning window
Streams of water forming patterns
Of a tapestry of drifting lines
That flow through my heart
Lines of hope
Lines of love
These transformative times
They all blend in the end
Into earth from where they came
To you Lord
I will remain.

I AM SO AWARE IN
THE EARLY HOURS
OF THE DAY,
IN ITS SILENCE,
HOW DEEP ARE
MY EMOTIONS OF
SHAME OF MY LIFE.
AND YET
I AM ALSO SO
CLOSE TO GOD I
HEAR HIS VOICE,
SO FULL OF LOVE
AND FORGIVENESS,
THAT I CRY EVERY
SINGLE MORNING.

A NEW VOICE

The day seems long
A texture of loneliness and loss
Seeps into my heart
Clouding my view of me
It is hard to let go
Of what we have failed to be
To see something new
To believe I can be
The voices that shame
Come in the silence of alone
Pulling me down to doubt
But a new Voice is growing
In the dark
Shining a light with a hope
Of rebirth
It is the Voice that called to Lazarus
In the dark
And it is the voice that is calling me
To come out
And to live again.

ON THE PATH AHEAD

I searched for a sign
Just beyond the bend
On the path ahead
Lengthening streams of sunlight
Stretch across my path
Daylight a mellowing goodbye
Offering a kiss of hope
I continue to seek
Where will the bend end
Darkness
The curtain closes the day
My steps cautiously proceed
Searching for the longing
On the path ahead.

ASK ME

There was a time I dreamed

Long ago

When I ran fast

Like a bolt of lightning

I felt I lit up the sky

I was a man

Young and spry

I was so

Alive

Ask Me of him

Let me tell you again

And help me remember

Of the man

I Remember I am.

OF TIME

I close my eyes
To awake my dreams
Like a white cloud
Gently sailing across a blue sky
I see time fading away
Lost in empty tombs
Of meaningless pursuits
I created in haste
Where God asks
Are you going?
Can't you see
The love I bring
Yet you chase these dead things
Where is your heart
Beware
Of time.

A SILENT TEAR

Alone is most quiet

In the dark early hours of night

Not a sound is heard

Except the cries

In a silent tear

The heart does not sleep

But beats

In its lonely cage

The longings of the broken heart offered here

In a Silent Tear.

I WAS JUST DOING MY MORNING WALK AND CONTEMPLATIVE PRAYER, AND I THOUGHT THIS TRUTH … "ALL THINGS END."

WHAT A POWERFUL TRUTH. EVERYTHING. JUST AS THE MORNING BIRTHS A NEW DAY… IT WILL EVENTUALLY FADE AS NIGHT COMES AND IT WILL END.

BUT TOMORROW MORNING A NEW DAY WILL COME AGAIN, AND I WILL EMBRACE IT WITH ALL MY HEART. FOR THIS DAY, THIS BEGINNING, IS ALL I HAVE TO SHARE WITH CHRIST AND MY LIFE.

SO I TAKE THE WISDOM AND ALL THE LOVE I LEARNED YESTERDAY AND I GO FORWARD AND LIVE IN THE FULLNESS OF THIS DAY. EVENTUALLY I WILL JOIN CHRIST IN THE UNDERSTANDING THAT HE IS MAKING ME NEW EACH AND EVERY MORNING.

SO I LET GO OF EVERYTHING… LET IT ALL GO.. LIVE TODAY IN MY REBIRTH… MY NEW BEGINNING… AND LOVE AND I BECOME ONE FOR THIS NEW DAY AND FOREVER IN ETERNITY. THIS IS A GROWTH MINDSET OF INTRINSIC HOPE.

I PROMISE YOU THIS

I have come a long distance
To find myself here with you
I have travelled many miles
And many years
Over many trails of tears
I have but a few remaining songs
That I can sing to you
I am all that remains
Of my fading dreams
But I will love you
With all my heart
For as long as I live
I promise you this.

INTO THE LIGHT

This path has appeared

It is where I have ended

It begins

Transcending the possible

A Light beams ahead

Into my darkness it calls

Offering a Hope

As Trust evolves

I step forward

Into the Light I go.

A VALLEY DOVE

I wandered through a valley
Following a dove
Its song called to my heart
So I followed on
Deep into its Forest
Of emerald green
With hope and a dream
I continued to proceed
There by a stream
She knelt down to drink
And turning to see
Our eyes did meet
Reaching for her hand
Her touch so sweet
I found my dream
A love to be.

FOLLOW THE DREAM

Whisper in the dark
A soft, lonely prayer

Gently let it sing
Its Melody of Hope

Arise my heart
Leave this sleeping tomb

Dare to dream again
Awaken my heart

Follow as it sings
Follow its beating wings
Follow the dream!

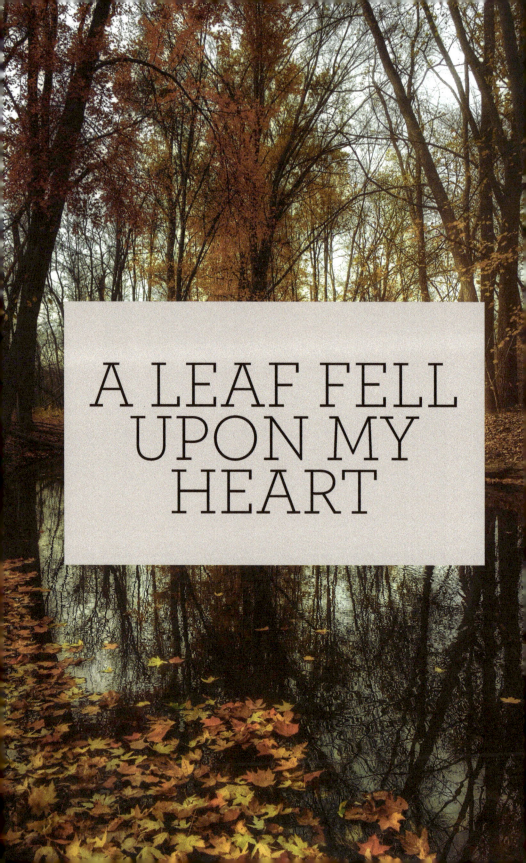

Down through a shady Grove
I walked among the trees
Aware of my lonely heart
With God I talked
A plea of mercy I brought
Sprung up from my soul
In search to believe
Suddenly, a rush of wind
Trembled through the trees
Whispering to me
I searched to see
As I looked above
A leaf fell upon my heart
Deep in my chest, I felt a beat
It's not too late
To begin again
To Love again
A leaf fell
Upon my heart.

CONTINUE YOUR JOURNEY

As you continue in pursuit of the person God created you to be, may you find these resources helpful, as well.

JOURNEY TO FREEDOM is a 36-day contemplative journey to help you understand your personal story and inner life more fully and compassionately. It will guide you through the stages needed for internal transformation, and allow you to find your own path toward emotional, spiritual and physical well-being.

JOURNEY OF TRANSFORMATION: CREATING THE LIFE YOU'VE ALWAYS WANTED is a 36-day contemplative journey to help you understand your personal story and inner life more fully and compassionately. It will guide you through the stages needed for internal transformation, and allow you to find your own path toward emotional, spiritual and physical well-being.

JOURNEY TO WHOLENESS takes the reader on a 42-day contemplative journey filled with compassion, introspection, meaningful connection, and true hope while navigating a breast cancer diagnosis. This book will guide you through grieving what you have lost and help you move into a place of wholeness. Collaboratively written, *Journey to Wholeness* is the passion project of fellow survivors who know the gift of TRUE community and connection in the process of healing.

JOURNEY TO A NEW BEGINNING AFTER LOSS helps heal the unacknowledged losses and disappointments in your life. From birth, you experience deeply profound losses that shape your story and circumstances. Your life is impacted by grief through intangible losses like unrealized dreams, unmet expectations, loss of innocence, trust, belonging, and self-worth. Or through tangible losses like finances, health, work, relationships, community, or death. Have you allowed yourself to truly grieve these losses? Do you feel that current losses bring up painful reminders of previous losses? Does lingering regret or resentment hold you back from a full life?

JOURNEY TO A LIFE OF SIGNIFICANCE helps you heal from the wounding of low self-worth. You may believe the lie that you will never be good enough, and so you strive to earn the love you long for and need. This book encourages honest self-reflection and movement toward acknowledging the inherent goodness and uniqueness God has placed in you. Uncover and examine the deeply rooted internal messages that hold you back from believing you are worthy, beloved or acceptable. Build a platform of self-worth to stand on that will positively impact all areas of your life.

PODCAST: Join us each week on the podcast *Searching Inward*.

WEBSITE: restoresmallgroups.org

YOUTUBE CHANNEL: *A Moment of Hope* – @AMomentofHope-nu5dx